T. E Ewen

How to Double the Wealth of Canada

T. E Ewen

How to Double the Wealth of Canada

ISBN/EAN: 9783337405168

Printed in Europe, USA, Canada, Australia, Japan

Cover: Foto ©Suzi / pixelio.de

More available books at **www.hansebooks.com**

HOW TO DOUBLE

-----THE-----

WEALTH OF CANADA,

Imperial Federation.

Continental · Union,

BY T. E. EWEN, M.A.

" To a Patriot the interests of his country are supreme."

PRINTED AT THE "DAILY ONTARIO" STEAM PRINTING HOUSE,
BELLEVILLE,

1893.

INTRODUCTION.

Only indisputable facts, conjoined with the most conclusive rguments, could have the power to change the political pro- livities of a descendant of the Canadian pioneers, who fought gainst the United States in 1812, and the Canadian Rebels in 1 1837-8.

The expatriation of my kindred first caused me to dare to hink. Ten years ago the writer received a sudden summons o attend the funeral of his favorite uncle, the last of his gen- ration. He left a widow and six stalwart sons. These sons /ere prosperous American citizens, scattered from Florida to lontana. I stood at his grave, the only male representative of our umerous race, born in Canada. Standing there I determined o ascertain the cause of the expatriation of my kin, and to do ly utmost to apply the remedy.

Rare opportunities for investigation were afforded me. I ravelled from Newfoundland to our North West, visiting every ity and almost every hamlet in our Dominion.

Many of our mines revealed to me their wealth. I travelled housands of miles in our lumber forests, and assisted in draw- ig in seines on all our great lakes. The language of our farms ; to me a mother tongue. I know and love Canada.

After years of study, the conclusion unwillingly arrived at ʹas :—The exile of my countrymen is caused by *Continental solation.* The remedy followed as a logical sequence.

I believe this little treatise only embodies in words the un- poken thoughts of many of my cautious, patient and unobtrusive ʒllow-citizens; men tenacious of old ideas; slow to move, but once ouvinced impossible to change or intimidate. This treaties is partial summary of my observations and conclusions. It ; small; but doubtless some wish it were smaller; disjointed, aving been written in time spared from business : incomplete, ozens of volumes would leave the subject unexhausted; but uch as it is, kindly extend to it your perusal and consideration.

T. E. EWEN.

BELLEVILLE, Jan., 1893.

ʹo all Canadian Patriots, and especially to the descendants of our Pioneers, I dedicate this little work.

THE HOMES OF CANADA.

Many Canadians adopt as their motto : " Man was made to mourn," and sit with folded hands and shaking heads, lamenting over the existing depression. Others prefer the manly utterance of Carlyle :—" Man was made to work," and energetically advocate which ever political policy they believe will be the most beneficial to the homes of Canada.

Canadians are essentially a race of energetic workers. This quality we have inherited from our forefathers, who in search of fortune, bid farewell to their trans-Atlantic homes, and crossed the ocean to live in Canada, then considered a frozen wilderness. Canada has a parentage of which she has every reason to be proud. Our forefathers, the pioneers of our country received their rugged but kindly land direct from the hands of the Great Architect of the Universe. These stalwart men faced danger with courage, cheerfully endured privations and isolation ; hewed their homes out of solitudes, and out of a wilderness—a no man's land—made their Canada. They made Canada. Canada was theirs. To their memory we first and foremost owe our allegiance. We, their descendants, inherited our Canada from them. Our dangers have been few, but we met them with courage. Our commercial privations, caused by continental isolation, have been many and great, but we have borne them hopefully. We cheerfully obey our laws because they are of our own making, having been enacted by legislators elected only by ourselves. We appoint our judges, hence our courts of justice are of our own creation. We are developing the resources of one of the fairest gifts to man, and supporting our Governments—not our governments us. Therefore Canada is solely ours, and if we are Canadian patriots, her welfare and interests are to us of paramount importance.

Individually we are toiling to support our homes. Home, with its hallowed and endearing associations, means more to the Anglo-Saxon and his kin than to the man of any other race. No language contains the equivalent of our word " Home." If it is morally right to benefit our homes, whose good is the chief object of our desires, and great incentive to our labors, then the political policy that will confer the greatest happiness and prosperity upon our homes is the one to manfully advocate. For, in the words of Burke,—" That which is morally right cannot be politically wrong."

Christmas witnesses re-united families, but in Canada at

many a Christmas dinner the son of the house was absent—a
exile in a foreign land.   How the dear old mother's eyes woul(
have brightened! how the father's hand would have claspe(
his! and how the children would have clustered around him i
the absent one had unexpectedly stepped in!   Can the policy
be wrong which would give this great joy to this family?   Con
tinental Union, by distributing the great attracting mercantile
and manufacturing industries equally   over all this Continent
will recall many of the absent sons and daughters of Can ida an(
prevent their departure in the future.   This would cause in
creased happiness in our homes ; hence, it must be not onl;
right, but our duty to thoroughly investigate this policy, usin;
the love of our homes as a lamp to lighten and guide our foot
steps.

FINANCIAL PROSPERITY.

Which political policy will confer the greatest financia
prosperity upon our Canadian homes ?

The reader will please bear in mind that the writer is no
to be reprehended on account of the following facts being in ex
istence :—

Britain acts honestly towards Canada, and as generously a
consistent with her own interests—nothing more.   Wheat
cheese and beef are our chief exports to Great Britain.   Bu
wheat, cheese and beef, of the same quality from Russia, th
United States or Canada always have, and always will com
mand, the same prices in the British markets.   Therefore, a
regards the amount of money we obtain from our transatlanti
exports, it is financially immaterial whether Canada is a par
of Russia, the United States or the British Empire.   Englanc
a workshop containing forty odd millions, does not, and dar
not, discriminate in favor even of her own food producers, muc
less of (urs. There fore our allegiance to Great Britain neither ha
nor will, financially benefit us on our exports to Europe.   A
for buying cheaply from Britain, that is not the questio1
Show us the policy that will provide us with more money, an
we will, like England, buy in the cheapest markets, or manu
facture the goods ourselves, free of duty on the American Cor
tinent.

Therefore, as British allegiance is of no money value t
Canada, on our exports to Britain, any political connection tha
will furnish us with more money from our exports elsewhere i

of more financial benefit to our homes. Our exports elsewhere consist principally of products sent to the markets of the United States, the chief of which are minerals, fish, lumber and farm produce. The policy which will obtain for us the most money from these sources of our wealth is therefore the one that will be, from a financial standpoint, the most beneficial to Canada. Continental Union is the policy that will provide the most money therefrom, consequently it is the best for us to advocate if we desire to increase the financial prosperity of our homes.

I.—MINERALS.

Canada contains every mineral except tin. The Canadian iron ore, containing less phosphorus than the American production, is the best on the continent; yet the United States' out-put is $50,000,000, and the Canadian out-put only the one-sixth of a million. One reason that the ratio of our ore is as 300 to 1 is, that the Canadian market, besides being too limited, has its centres of population so far apart that the cost of transportation exceeds the profits. Other causes are, the American duty on Canadian ore, and the proposed Canalian export duty on some minerals. The American duties on iron ore and bituminous and lignite coal are 75 cents a ton, and ½ cent per lb. on the copper contained in its ore. Capitalists, whether British, American or Canadian, are thorough citizens of the world, and would not long be capitalists if they did not regard business matters solely from their financial standpoints. Hence, they wisely refuse to operate Canadian mines in preference to American, when the mines and the markets would be in different countries ; and their heavy immovable investments would be subject to the poverty, cupidity, caprice or antagonism of either government.

In nickel and copper, Sudbury and Lake Superior districts are unrivalled. There is only one other nickel mine in the world, known to, and utilized by, modern science for commercial purposes. Look at our undeveloped mineral wealth. The ridges of copper at Sudbury are actually miles long. In Canada, only four miles from Lake Superior there is one mountain nugget of pure copper one thousand feet thick, which if it were situated only a few miles to the south, in the United States, would be worth fifteen million dollars. The amount of visible copper in that region is incalculable, but situated where it is, it is all utterly valueless. We know the reason. Britain does not want it, for her ocean vessels can load at the equally unexhaustible copper mines of Newfoundland. The United States does not want it, for they have copper inside their ring of nations, and outside of that ring they never unnecessarily go for supplies of raw material.

Let us form an idea of what ought to be in Canada, from what is transpiring in the immediate vicinity, but unfortunately across the line. Let us ascertain the profits of just two mines, on the American side of Lake Superior. During the last 30 years they have paid to their owners an annual profit above all

iderably above $1,00),000. Picture what hives
ld be created around all those mineral treasur-
ontinental Union supplying the needed enter-
l markets. And then estimate, if you can, the
e direct benefits that would result to our poo-
osperity and happiness that would consequent-
homes. Canada, my country! why continue
enact the part of Tantalus, and the unattain-
ng draught? The *role* is neither wise nor
,inly is both cruel and unjust to those whose
ly entrusted to your care.
al criterion of the mechanical advancement and
nation is not its yearly crop of politicians, but
pita consumption of iron ore. The amount of
s mines is not necessarily identical with its in-
ion. The nation whose *per capita* use of iron
i the world is the United states. Although it
per cent. of the earth's population, yet it con-
one-third of the world's iron, steel, lead,and cop-
f its coal, and one-half of its tin. Therefore,
is the best mineral market on this globe. In
mineral exports were only about $5,000,000, of
tanding the duties, the United States took 80
American capitalist, having plenty of minerals
try, does not work foreign mines under adverse
also necessary to pay a duty to get the miner-
erican markets. Hence, the Bruce mines are un-
most in wi thsight,in the United States, 7 million
copper ores were taken out in 1889, worth at
)0,000, and at the point of delivery $35,000,000,
,000,000 for lake freights.
admitted by Governor Andrews, of Mass., that
American Union, Nova Scotia, having now the
i, coal, and flux in proximity, would, with the
s of the adjacent markets of New England,
t excel, Pennsylvania in great iron industries.
Quebec are fleeing from the banks of our
wrence as if its shores were plague stricken.
the Eastern States welcome them as the ma-
ich to form the best of operatives. In future
vould find congenial employment, without being
s a free American state, Nova Scotia would also
iantities of coal from her inexhaustable mines

to the bordering New England States which
coal. In Nova Scotia, seven hundred feet un
writer saw mines work eight hours for 60 cent
then receive men's wages for men's work.

Here is a startling fact :—In the North
and British Columbia the deposits of lignite
coal are larger than all England, and only C
will furnish, as an abundant and assuredly per
the whole of the American Pacific coast.

Basing our calculations upon the well-k
Wisconsin and Michigan employ one-fourth of
Canada, with Continental Union, will have in
one-fourth of a million additional miners, a
eighth of a million men employed in iron and
tories—equal to an additional population of ne
If we suppose that under Continental Union t
mineral exports for all Canada will only equal
states of the Union, Michigan and Wisconsin
yearly increased out-put of $25,000,000. If w
present exports, it will g ve a total of $30,0
Our present export of $5,000,000 is comparat
ty. No country in the world is richer in min
significance of our present mineral exports is
our suicidal Continental isolation. Continenta
us freely, fully and perpetually, the nearest a
market in the world.

Two men will not enter into a contract
modities unless each considers he is receiving i
equal value. Commercial treaties between
contracts of exchange to their mutual ad
basis of giving and receiving equal benefits
treaties will not be satisfactory or permanent.
membered that the American Government is c
triotic business men who desire every commer
to the advantage of their country. Consequentl
no treaty with Canada when the advantage is
favor. Our iron being free from phosphorus
theirs for the manufacture of the higher grades
If our minerals were permanently admitted f
consequences would be that many of their mi
operations, and thousands of men and millions
be transferred to Canada. In fact, almost
would derive from our minerals or from the

r taken from the United States. Therefore, as
erals, it would be an act of the most consum-
e part of the United States to enter into a
.y with Canada, which would be solely to the
ountry. The Americans, most assuredly, will
dvantages they possess within their Union to
ot desire to benefit their country, who do not
; it up or maintaining its laws, and whose only
iggrandizement at its expense. This is not
course pursued by a nation whose first and only
welfare of its own people. Consequently, the
y which Canada can obtain an equal share
of the wealth to be derived from her minerals
unity of interests. This means Continental

food exports to Great Britain, of wheat, cheese
not be sufficient to feed the two million ad-
nts that the opening of the American markets
would give us.

II.—FISHERIES.

sheries of Canada are among the richest and
in the world, while the Fresh Water Fisheries
es are nowhere to be surpassed, the total
in 1891, was about $20,000,000. Here again,
es is our best market. The duty, however, being
e fishermen, wherever possible unfurled their
d to the American flag and have their homes
l. in order to enter their fish free of duty. This
the fact that out of the total annual Lake
500,000, Canadian vessels captured less than
tinental Union is the only policy that
fishermen to permantly locat their homes
the best fishing grounds, which are gen-
he Canadian shores. Continental Union
abolish the American duty on fish when
ladians. These duties at present hive the
e American shores. Political Union would
of the fishermen of Lake Erie to be equally
y distributed along both the Canadian and
; therefore, in all probability they would both
tities of fish, which would be $1,750,000 each.

This would be three times the present Lake Erie catch of t
Canadian fishermen. If we apply this rule to the catch of
Ontario, it would increase the annual catch of fish caught
those living on Canadian shores and sailing vessels built in C
nada by $6,000,000. If, in order to be certain to be within t
bounds of reasonable probability, we only assert that Continer
al Union will increase the catch of the fish of all Canada to t
extent that it would probably benefit one province, we ha
still an annual financial increase to our wealth of $6,000,000.

III.—SHIP BUILDING AND LAKE FREIGHTS.

Canada, besides thousands of miles of sea coast, has t
largest and most important system of inland navigation in t
world, as illustrated by Port Arthur and Liverpool being almo
equidistant from our Atlantic ports.

Canada having timber which is in requisition the wo₁
wide for ship building, we would naturally expect that t
American Clyde would be in Canada. But it is at Clevelar
where, in 1891, new vessels were built having a tonnage
71,000, which was 17,000 more tonnage than built in all Ca₁
da. On the Great Lakes during 1892 there were building
the American side 50 steel steamers of 2,000 to 3,000 tons ea
and on the Canadian side, only two steamers of 200 tons. O₁
one per cent. of the first-class shipping on the Great Lakes
Canadian. In 1892 the the total tonnage that passed throu
the Canadian Welland Canal was less than one million, a gr₁
part of which was American through freight from Duluth a
Chicago to American Lake Ontario ports. Whereas the freig
that passed through the American Sault Ste Marie Canal v
over ten million tons, and that which passed by Detroit was
million tons, only one per cent. of which was carried in Ca₁
dian bottoms. No comments are necessary.

The principal reasons for this deplorable condition are
follows :—

The United states do not allow Canadian vessels to ca₁
freights from one American port to another. The Ameri₁
doties do not permit of a large trade in heavy freights fr
Canada to the Unsted States. The only present ou₁
from our North West is by means of the Canadian Pacific; ₁
this railroad takes good care that no freights entrusted to
leave its line, so as to proceed from Port Arthur, by the oth
wise cheaper lake routes. Continental Union is the only pol

lish every one of these serious and unjust disad-
· marine interests of Canada.
ity of our young Canadians, as soon as they be-
ed seamen, move to the United States, and be-
citizens, because only American citizens are per-
1 American vessels. It is to their interest to do
ie Americans pay far better wages. An able
from 25 to 35 per cent. and an officer from 20 to
her salary than he would receive if he sailed in
sel.
unnual value of the Great Lakes' freight and
now about $45,000,:00. When this $45,000,-
paid out, Canada is conspicuous by receiving
),000. Only Political Union will enable her to
share of it.
ted portion of Eastern Canada possesses accord--
nore miles of navigable water than any part of
ontinent,—in fact it is the Britain of America.
ean and the Gibraltar of this Continent belong
cean outlet of the Great Lakes is ours. Though
1 lavish with us, yet, on account of our foolish
ores are comparatively shipless.
ierican side of the Great Lakes prosperity and
gone hand in hand. They have enlarged the
pper lakes at great expense, but their wealthy
no burden. The construction of the Sault Ste
·flects credit upon the American nation, and its
·ls that of the outlet of the Mediterranean to In-
uez Canal. The reason the Republic has not, at
, improved the navigation of the lower lakes is
: not possess the St. Lawrence River, the outlet

.l Union would transform our shores, for the
rnment has even now in contemplation that, if
are united, they would deepen and widen all the
he largest ocean vessels could sail direct from
·rt Arthur to London and Liverpool. This would
ke and river ports, in reality, ocean ports. The
: immense, for much of the soil in the neighbor·
eat Lakes is unsurpassed in the world for fertili-
l wealth is unequalled; and the prairies of the far
.heir golden grain in millions of bushels. The
.1 ing and mercantile centres of the earth would

be along our inland waters, and the commerce of the Medite
ranean would be small in comparison with that of our Grea
Lakes.

IV.—LUMBER.

The amount of timber annually cut in Canada is immens
This fact may be realized from the gigantic figures necessary t
use when speaking of even that part of the production of ou
forests which we export. In 1890, among the exports wei
1,500,000,'0') feet of sawed logs, 5,500,000 cubic feet of squai
timber, and 1,000,' 00 railroad ties. Besides these there we
exported immense quantities of hard-wood lumber, cord-woo
pulp-wood, tan-bark, shingles, posts, telegraph poles, etc.

The United States, having less timber *per capita* than eve
Germany, is our great market The duty, however, varies fro
$1.00 to $2.50 per 1,000 feet. This duty caused the Canadia
to contribute to the revenue of the Great Republic betwee
1865 and 1890 $20,000,000 in order that access might be gaine
for our lumber to the markets of this continent. The resul
from the American duty and the great cost to send the lumb
to any other country, is that it only remunerates us to saw in
lumber for export the choicest logs out of each tree that is c
down. Consequently, millions of dollars worth of inferi
logs are annually left to rot in our timber limits, as the write
eyes have seen.

Basing our calculations upon the above giant figures, ai
remembering that our exports of $23,633,675 annually, only r
present that part of the felled timber which is remunerati
under existing circumstances, we cannot place the unnecessai
yearly waste of our inferior lumber at less than $2,000,000 a
nually. Continental Union is the only policy that will pe
manently give Canada all the adjacent markets of this Contine
free of duty. This will enable her to obtain remunerati
prices for her inferior grades of pine and hard-wood lumb
and timber, now not worth paying the duty on and exportin
This waste and loss would then cease, and we would effect a
annual saving of at least $2,000,000 worth of the products
our forests, now allowed to rot on account of the duty debarri
them from free admission to the near markets of the Unit
States.

A perusal of the trade and navigation report for 1892, 1
veals the following facts, well worthy of the attention of tl
inhabitants of the Province of Ontario :—

the total exports, the products of this Province,
),915,939, of which $460,000 were from our
) from our mines, $8,332,000 from our forests,
our farms, and only $3,404,000 from our fac-

tal exports of thirty millions of dollars, the
otwithstanding the restrictions imposed upon
million dollars worth, and Britain with the
of free trade markets only 11¼ million dollars
58 per cent. to the United States and only 38
in.
s revive our faith in the accuracy of the faded
inada that hung on the walls of the old school-
hood.
of Ontario was there depicted, not as a part of
ing snugly wedged in between the states of
lichigan, and with them forming the center of
of the Continent of North America. •
ie, the United States bought all the lumber
trio, and this lumber formed one-half of the
his province to the Republic.   -
g timber was not the product of the labor and
her does nature produce it rapidly. Canadians
quickly and recklessly our grand forests are
. The government, satisfied with collecting
picest timber, allows the rest to rot or to be
ith the very soil which could, if preserved only
reafter, reproduce it. No generation is now en-
this timber than nature produces during the
generation, and any infringment upon this rule
the rights of our descendants, and an over-
capital entrusted to our province.
legislators of Ontario pose as paragons of po-
nd economy.
consider the trustee who recklessly used up
and the capital of a valuable estate, belonging
be either honest, economical or truthful when
re me for I have managed the estate well. We
How the minors of that estate would at their
at trustee.
governments have connived at and shared in
d from the wholesale and reckless destruction
itage of the future generations of Canadians.

They have lived upon the capital of our Province and not upon its legitimate income. The great source of their income, the forest part of our capital will soon be gone,—and what then ?

Foreseeing this approaching deficiency in the revenue, an attempt was made by our provincial legislatures to duplicate their forest method upon our mineral wealth, by means of royalties and export duties, with the result, that these infant industries were nipped in the bud, and all capitalists were thus made cognizant of the existence of the above facts, and the resultant danger to taxable investments in Ontario.

The consequence is, that no capitalist feels safe in investing any large amount of money in working mines in Ontario under our existing Provincial Government.

Besides the waste of our timber, there is another great loss in our lumber business on account of continental isolation. The United States need our timber, but at the same time desire to obtain all the employment possible for their citizens. Consequently, they allow logs to enter their country free of duty,— but they put a duty of $1.00 per 1,000 feet on roughly sawn boards, and a higher duty of $2.50 per 1,000 on all boards that are plained and groved, and still a higher duty on all lumber that is more highly finished. The result is, that Canada is a hewer of wood, and the United States saw, plane and finish. To prove this, the Spanish River district furnished 140,000,000 feet of unsawn logs to the United States; and three quarters of the logs that were sawed last year at the extensive mills at Bay City and Saginaw, Michigan, were from Canada. Where it is impossible to export it altogether free of duty in the crude shape of logs, it is sawn in Canada into rough boards, and these are sent to the United States at the lowest possible duty. These rough boards are then planed and finished in the United States by thousands upon thousands of American workmen.

Continental Union would change all this. The bulk and freight is far less when the lumber is sawn and finished. Labor is cheaper in Canada, and our water powers are more numerous and more conveniently situated for this work. Consequently, if there were no duties between us and our American markets, almost all the lumber would be sawn and finished in Canada. As the result of this new demand for labor, it has been carefully estimated by an Ottawa lumber king, that, when continental union is consummated, the population of his city will immediately increase one-half. What would be true of Ottawa would also be true of many of our other towns and hamlets

ly increase our prosperity, and also furnish
nany thousands who are now annually com-
eir Canadian homes. Our hardy and skillful
iver-drivers are universally acknowledged by
ellers to be the best men in the world at their
ese fearless sons of toil would then obtain con-
it in our numerous mills and factories when
lent, rheumatism or old age. Only political
the United States to take the duty off the
nd thus relinquish this great source of wealth
would then be their sister.
ho aspire to the dignity of Canadian states-
o solve this problem. Whether is it better to
that will furnish employment for Canadians
a, and have other nations pay us for the fin-
our labor ? Or to remain as we are—merc-
of raw material, the hewers of wood for for-

V—CANADIAN EXILES.

he fate of Spain ! Drained of her young blood,
, and from a first-class power fell to a third.
ts are chiefly in families, therefore emigration
her. Our emigrants are principally young
, intellectually or physically, no nation can
A nation, whose policy annually expatriates
young men, must eventually deteriorate both
sically, because the powerful leave, and the
f its population remain. The effects of a policy
more detrimental to a country than a pestil-
for these carry off principally the weak and
sing the case, it is the solemn duty of every
le all minor and baser motives and consult in
with his brother Canadians, how best the
more injurious to his country than pestilence
stopped. This exodus of our youth is a fatal
ty of our nation; therefore, we must remember
esperate diseases require desperate remedies,
acious remedy is better than the consequences
Let us be patriots to our beloved Canada,
cts squarely and unflinchingly, and immedia-
nedy that our reason tells us will be the most

certain and permanent. It is both wrong and foolish for us to allow the ephemeral politics of the hour, or prejudices concerning the distant or the past, to militate against the present welfare of our homes and Canada.

Those who do not wish to recognize the depression existing in Canada, as the cause of the present exodus, say that there has always been a drift of population from the colder to the milder climates ; and that as soon as the Middle States are filled, there will be a reflux of emigration to Canada. This is true to only the most limited extent. Our young men are the sons of hardy sires. These sires, in search of homes and fortune left the milder climate of Britain to come to what was then considered a frozen wilderness. Our young men, like their forefathers, seeing little hope of success at home go where fortune favors. If the brightest prospects of success on this continent were 200 miles north of their Canadian homes there they would go. Success they are determined to achieve difficulties, even dangers, are only an incentive to action. 1 the chances of success in Canada and the States were equal they would prefer to reside in Canada. Converse with the next ten Canadian emigrants you meet, and be convinced tha effeminacy is not a characteristic of our countrymen. To furthe prove this, our youth settle in parts of the United States that ar on an average as cold as their Canadian homes; and this, toc when Florida and Southern California would welcome them a readily as Michigan or Dakota.

The emigration from Canada to the States is about three hundred daily. This includes both those born in Canada and in foreign countries.

The population of the three counties adjoining the county in which the writer's home is situated, have decreased 12 pe cent. during the last ten years. Then contrast this fact:—Th three states bordering on his province have increased in popula tion during the same time as follows :—New York, three-quar ters of a million ; Ohio and Michigan half a million each.

Chicago, during the same time, increased more in wealt and population than all Canada, and to-day contains more Ca nadians than any city in the Dominion, west of Montreal, with the single exception perhaps of Toronto. Detroit has a population of 260,000. Windsor, with equal shipping facilities, and with fou railroads entering it, has only 10,000. Seventeen years ag Manitoba and Dakota started even, with 14,000 whites each to-day Dakota contains more people than the Dominion car boast of between Ottawa and the Pacific Ocean. In many counties of Dakota the first question that one naturally asks a stranger is, " Well, what part of Canada did you come from ?"

Isolate any one of the States of the American Union from the rest of this Continent, and its fate will be similar to that of Canada.

Continental Union, by distributing the attracting factories and mercantile enterprises equally over this Continent, opening up our mines, and giving us our rightful number of fishermen, ship-builders and sailors, will increase the population of Canada several millions. We would retain at least 30,000 men out of the many thousand more who annually leave us to assist in building up the great country to the south. A man on an average pays into the revenue of his country $1,000 during his life-time in direct and indirect taxation. Thirty thousand Canadians retain each year hereafter, at $1,000 *per capita*, is $30,000,000 annually. If we confine our attention to the amount of revenue the United States obtains by means of taxes alone, from these 30,000 Canadians, it declares that Canada makes the United States a yearly gift, equivalent to $30,000,00). No wonder Canada is poor when she has thus been aiding the United States to rapidly pay off their national debt. If we capitalize this $30,000,000 at four per cent. per annum, it is equivalent to a capital of $750,000,000. In other words, if Canada wished to deposit a sum of money so that the interest thereof, at four per cent. per annum, would be equivalent to the value of this annual exodus, she would require to deposit $750,000,000.

VI—IMMIGRATION.

The emigrant from Europe is generally a man dissatisified with kingly rule ; consequently, not desirous of becoming again a subject, even of her most Gracious Majesty, but wishes to be the monarch of himself. Even of the total British emigration of 1890, the United.States got 80 per cent.

Being a part of an Empire, is the principal reason that the emigrant from the Continent of Europe avoids Canada. Because, all kingdoms and empires, Britain included, for their own jealous interests, have mutually enacted, that taking the oath of allegiance to a foreign potentate, does not free any man from military servitude to the land of his nativity. The German

and Scandinavian emigrant, when leaving his home and fathe
land, has a firm intention to revisit them, but he desires to
able to return from America, without the fear of being in
pressed into a European army. He knows that the foreig
born American citizen is almost the only man, who can wa
the streets of his native European town without the dread
conscription. Consequently, the European wisely emigrates
the American Republic, and not to a part of the British Er
pire. There is also on the Continent of Europe, among th
Germans and Scandinavians, the same jealous aversion again
all things English, that some Canadians have against th
Americans.

Canada has only retained 19,000 out of the 800,000 imm
grants that she has imported from Europe during the last to
years, at a cost to her, of between $3,000,000 and $4,000,00
The immigrants have accepted the assisted passages offere
by Canada to aid them to reach the United States. Hence
each immigrant that Canada retained cost her nearly $20
which was just $199.99 more than some of them were worth
any country.

The United States immigration was, at the close of th
American war, 750,000 annually. During the last few yea
the Republic has rejected the undesirable applicants for admi
sion to her country, and thus restricted the immigration to 500,00
a year. Unlike Canada, it did not desire to import ment
moral and physical contaminations from the slums of the citi
of Britain or the Continent, even if they paid their own pass
ages. The States have now only a small quantity of first-cla
land to offer to settlers which does not require expensiv
irrigation.

Canada posseses great undeveloped mineral wealth an
large areas of unoccupied and fertile land; therefore, und
Continental Union, she will be the part of the new confederac
that will be specially boomed. Many of the present inhabit
ants of the United States will then inmigrate to Eastern Car
ada, and develop our mines, and find employment in new man
facturing industries. There will also be a large influx from th
Western States to the generous prairies of our North West. I
addition, Canada will obtain a great part, if not the great
part, of the large immigration that naturally tends from north
ern Europe to America. Continental Union is the only powe
that will cause the effective American immigration agency to boo
Canada, to fill up our North West, to realize the dream of 2

)orders, and to find lucrative employment for
're limit this annual stream of immigration to
ericans, Britons, Scandinavians and Germans, it
enormous addition to Canada's wealth. She
om each of them on an average $1,000 dur-
e by means of direct and indirect taxation.
immigrants yearly at $1,000 each is $40,000,000

n Governments must consider immigration to be
ey have spent many millions of dollars upon this
vocates of Continental Union have an immigra-
bmit to the the approval of the voters of Can-
e of the most advantageous and gigantic that
fered to the consideration of any country in the
 present government could induce the entire
ance to settle in Canada, and bring all their
h them, they would neither, in population or
the advantages offered by this policy. If the
o induced the whole population of Norway,
l and Belgium to emigrate to Canada and bring
ins and fertile vales with them, all these would
balance. If in despair, our government com-
and, Portugal, Turkey-in-Europe and Greece,
rritories and populations, to also move to Can-
ns belonging to many nationalities, would now
 population that Continental Union offers
; this supposed immigration would possess a
parable defect. The population would not be
vn, and we would never be able to assimilate
llions, for we cannot even assimilate the pres-
f Canada.
iate immigration that Continental Union offers
5,000,000, not of foreigners, but of our own
at home in our own continent. Many genera-
way, before Europe will offer to Canada a simi-
immigrants.
tion of the United States consumes more *per*
the necessities and luxuries of life, than any
pe, and the Republic possesses more men who
ite than any trans-Atlantic nation. But some
,000 do not live in Canada. This is true, but
them live nearer Canada than the Provinces
. Their people are also more similar to the

Canadians who reside in the contiguous Provinces, than the populations of the distant parts of Canada are to each other. New York State is nearer to Ontario than Prince Edward Island, and the people are also more similar. The inhabitants of Manitoba and Dakota are almost identical, and only a road separates them:—But British Columbia and Quebec are far asunder in the characteristics of their people, as they are distant in territory. Carefully consider whether it is better to accept our relatives the United States of Britons, about whom we know the best and the worst; or to take 65 million immigrants from Europe to our bosom, about whom we know little, and that little often in their disfavor?

VII--DUTIES.

We pay $6,000,000 annually in duties to the United States in order to get our products to their markets. Only Continental Union will entirely and permanently remove this barrier to commerce, and payment of tribute to the revenues of the United States without any corresponding benefit to Canada.

VIII—CUSTOM HOUSES AND DOMINION GOVERNMENT.

The great extent of the dividing line between Canada and the United States, a patrol of 4,000 miles, and the ample facilities thus afforded for smuggling, necessitates both governments maintaining an army of custom officials. It is stated by the Government of the United States, regarding her custom houses bordering on Canada, that the cost of collection, compared to the amount collected, is disproportionately large, in comparison with any other part of her revenue. This is also true in Canada. Continental Union will dismiss the majority of the officers now belonging to the Canadian custom houses bordering on the United States, and allow them to add by useful labor to the wealth of their respective provinces.

The internal government of our provinces will not be perceptibly changed by Continental Union. The Provincial governments will remain almost unchanged, and, in addition to their present legislation, they will perform a great part of that now done at Ottawa. The Dominion Government, with its useful, ornamental and expensive adjuncts, now numbers over 350 salaried members and officials, either employed or lounging around the Parliament buildings at Ottawa. Continental Union will promote about 40 of these to a higher and larger sphere of action, and permit over 300 to retire to private life, adding thereby to their own and the nation's wealth.

The saving that will be effected by Continental Union in the Department of Customs and the Dominion Government will exceed $1,000,000 annually. This saving can only be effected by Continental Union, for the most vivid imagination cannot conceive of the Governor General, High Commissioner, Senate, —in short, of 300 of the members and salaried officials at Ottawa, disbanding themselves just for the good of Canada; still less of them, dismissing the majority of their *useful* lieutenants in the Customs Department, to earn honest bread Many of those persons who would be dismissed are estimable as private individuals. Lut, in their present positions they are a great and useless expense—a tax and restriction upon commerce; consequently an. injury to us and to the prosperity of Canada.

IX—CANADIAN DEBT.

The Dominion and Provincial debts, amounting now to at least $260,000,000, will be assumed under Continental Union by the new Confederacy. Canada then will pay her *per capita* share of the total debts of the new nation. This $260,000,000, although now $52 *per capita* to our Canadian population, will be, under Continental Union, less than $4 *per capita* to the new confederacy of 70 million people. The present United States debt is $10 *per capita* which, added to the $4 as above, will give $14 as the debt *per capita* to the new Confederacy. Then the debt, to 5 million Canadians at $14 *per capita*, will be a total of $70,0 0,000, instead of our present $260,000,000. This would represent a saving of $190,000,000 to Canada. Nothing but Continental Union will cancel this large amount of our indebtedness. This debt, if it annually increases as in the past, will eventualy crush us.

X—REAL ESTATE.

The total value of the real estate of the Canadian people is not in the Canadian year book, but the wealth of all Canada is stated to be $4,765,000,000. Hence, the probable value of the real estate is at least $3,200,000,000.

Tax sales, vacant houses, and deserted farms speak of a

lack of population in Canada. Our unworked mines and ship-less shores tell of a lack of markets for heavy freights under existing circumstances. The comparison of quotations for agricultural products here and in the adjoining States pro-claims continental isolation. These are the chief causes of the depreciation in the values of real estate, too keenly felt to re-quire comment.

Continental Union, by increasing the population, volume of trade, and wealth from mine, sea, field and forest, will cause the value of real estate to advance at least 25 per cent. through-out the Dominion. This will effect a gain to Canada of $800,-000,000 in real estate values. During the boom you would doubtless unload a few choice corner lots.

XI—AGRICULTURE.

Last, but greatest of all comes the industry of agricul-ture. Out of our population of 4,829,411—56 per cent, or 2,704,470, derive their living from our farms. This gives Canada considerably over half a million farmers. A comparison of the market reports of the similarly situated Canadian and Ameri-can markets, reveals the deplorable fact, that our farmers only receive two-thirds of the price obtained by the American farm-ers, for the two-thirds of our agricultural products, for which our continent is the natural, and consequently the best market. Farmers, take your pencils and figure each for himself the amount you lose each year on account of being deprived of your rightful share of the markets of this continent. Recollect you not only lose on what you send to the States, but also on the same classes of your products when you sell them in Canada. We are safe in stating that $2.00 per acre each year is a very moderate figure at which to average this loss. The number of acres under actual cultivation is on an average 50 acres to each Canadian farmer, making a total of 25 million acres. A loss of $2.00 per acre means a loss to Canada each year of $50,-000,000 on the products of agriculture. Only Continental Union will permanently prevent this loss. Is not a Canadian farmer as much of a man as an American? Do not his labors deserve equal remuneration?

It having been proved that Continental Union will increase
e happiness and prosperity of our homes, more than any
her political policy, let Canadians, by all constitutional and
eaceful means, promote its adoption ; but only upon equal and
onorable terms, and with the consent of Great Britain. Let
s advocate it kind y but firmly and persistently.

SUCCESS IS INEVITABLE.

Continental Union.

————o————

Canadian rea ler, when considering this subject your m
is paramountly influenced by one of three sentiments:

BRITISH PATRIOTISM :

HATRED OF THE UNITED STATES, OR

CANADIAN PATRIOTIS

Please carefully classify yourself before proceeding.

————o————

BRITISH PATRIOTISM.

A ZOLLVEREIN OF THE BRITISH NATIONS IS DECLARED
HISTORY TO BE INEVITABLE.

————————

A love of Unity and Freedom is characteristic of
British race.

Of all the nations of the world England has always led
the van of freedom. Scotland, whose heath a con queror nev
trod, united with England, Ireland and Wales in forming i
united kingdom of Great Britain and Ireland. On the un
of the races the isles prospered as no other European nat

has. The people multiplied, until the land could not con-
their millions, then the restless and daring among
bid farewell to their homes and crossed the Atlantic.
in, kind and generous, forgot for a moment the love of the
for freedom, and was rigorous with her transAtlantic
ring. The colonies, loving freedom as well as the parent,
v off the restraining hand. The spirit of unity still guid-
our race prompted the thirteen colonies to unite in one
le—the United States of Britons. Since then the rapidity
vastness of their prosperity has amazed the world. The
erland has not since attempted to infringe upon the liber-
of her children.
Britain, had also other colonies transplanted world wide,
hom the spirit of unity so prevailed, that they have re-
d their allegiance to her even when to their financial in-
Six colonies of Britons dotted the coast of the continent
istralia; the spirit of unity breathed upon them, and they are
lidating themselves into one Commonwealth—a name singu-
appropriate. Seven small isolated provinces were scat-
along 4,000 miles across America; in answer to the same
hey became one Dominion. The history of our race is a
d of amalgamations. We have seen they have been made
every possible occasion from the dawn of old Anglo-
n history to the union of our Dominion.
What do all these unions declare? Remember history re-
itself. We are the descendants in the characteristics of
as well as in those of body, of the men who in times
consolidated weak clans and hostile tribes into a great na-
at whose warlike array Europe trembled. It is therefore
rent to the student of history, that unless prevented, a
Zollverein of the Anglo-Saxons of the world will be form-
ith Britain, the old motherland in the center ;—clustering
id her will be her children,—the free British nations of
earth,—the greatest of which will be United North
ica.
Now, British patriot, in the interests of our race heed the
of unity, whose promptings have been the cause of our
r and prosperity. This dominant family has only two
ions ; Britain with her colonies, and the United States of
ns. The connecting link is Canada. Upon Canada rests
esponsibility of creating between them constant discord or
tual peace. Under existing circumstances constant dis-
is declared by history to be inevitable. History is given

us for entertainment, instruction, and especially for warni
In all its ages and all its languages it reiterates the danger
man making two nations out of what the Almighty created
be one.   One nation should include all those who live wit
the same great natural boundries of mountains or oceans, w
speak the one language, have the same faith, obey the sa
laws and are of the one blood.   Canada and the United Sta
were form rly one people, and are yet identical in all the
quisites to be again one nation ; even their laws are upon
common basis of the English laws ; hence, in remaining ap
they are breaking one of nature's laws.   Penalties are invar
bly and wisely attached to the infraction of any of His gr
laws of nature.   The penalty attached to the breaking of t
law is jealousy with all its resultant evils.   This is proved
every divided nation in every age.   Let us confine ourselves
our own race and watch the effects.   The history of the ch
of Scotland and the heptarchy of England is written in blo
Unions brought internal peace.   On their consolidation i
separate kingdoms, England no sooner waged war on the c
tinent than Scotland crossed the borders.   Pillage and blo
shed pointed out the track of her raiders.   Then, England
turning in her might devastated the lowlands of Scotla
Union conferred peace, good fellowship and prosperity.   T
war of 1812 was model e l upon the former history of our r
Britain was again at war in Europe, and the United Sta
vainly attempted to wrest Canada from her.   To-day jealo
resorts to war between the divided nation in America,—a w
of tariffs, the next to bloodshed, and often culminating in blo
shed.   Union will confer peace and plenty as in the past.   W
ever aids in maintai ing or fostering the jealousies betwe
Canada and our relatives to the South, is guilty of attempti
to injure both Canada and Britain ; therefore he is not a patr
either to Canada, Old England, or his race, but a traitor
them all.   This union of the Anglo-Saxon, first of America, a
then, of the world is inevitable, because it is in accordance w
the noblest characteristics of our race, and a fulfilment of c
of His laws of nature.

Canada will soon attain her majority, and not remain u
der the guardianship of England, but become an independe
nation.   This will cause her to attain more of the distinctic
of a separate nation, whereas now she is in a plastic conditi
Our prosperity will in the meantime be retarded, conseque
ly the union will be upon less advantageous terms and har

of accomplishment. The union will not then furnish reasons for gratitude toward Britain on the part of either nation. Whereas now, if the union be effected, Canada will feel grateful to the mother who, to benefit her daughter, sanctioned her union with her prosperous relative. The United States will also feel grateful to the motherland for the further gift of Canada. The friendship between the Anglo-Saxons, whose shores are laved by the Atlantic, will then endure until time is no more.

British patriots, the advocates of Continental Union are in your ranks, and will advocate no policy that will not benefit England, Canada, and our race at large. The consideration of this policy will be laid at the foot of the British throne. Our beloved Queen and her wise councillors will deside upon it. When it receives their sanction and that of the parliaments of Canada and Britain and the Congress of America, then it must be loyal to adopt it. That it will be sanctioned is certain, for all the events of the past point in this direction. Why else did Britain in 1815 cede to the United States domain enough for an empire,—a strip 300 miles wide across America from ocean to ocean ? Why else than to aid her child in her financial trouble did she gives her $15,500,000 at the close of the American war ? Why has she in every treaty favored the United States, —except that, she considers the prosperous Republic as her well-beloved first-born, and that in benefiting her she, is entrusting to the hands of a wise guardian the heritage of the race in America, including that of Canada ?

FINANCIAL BENEFITS TO BRITAIN.

The majority of our Canadian families are more nearly allied to the inhabitants of the United States than to those of Great Britain, yet Britain is the land we love best after Canada, though we pay nothing to her revenues,—the only bond of unity being amity and trade. Our purchases from the British Islands are some $40,000,000 annually. with a profit to Britons, personally unknown to us, of $4,000,000, just a *ten cent piece* profit to each one of Britain's 40,000,000 inhabitants. British patriot, in this practical age be practical, and not a dreamer of antiquated phantasies, that are utterly devoid of any pecuniary value. Realize that only in proportion as a political policy enriches Canada, will it be in the power of Canada by her increased trade to financially benefit England. Canadians are

never niggards with their money. Only Conti
by increasing our numbers and purchasing powe
us to financially benefit Britain. This can only
increase of legitimate trade, flowing in natural,
channels. The benefits the motherland obtains
are solely derived from the profits she realizes on
from her.

We cannot buy from Britain without mone
say, we send England cheese for example, and sh
us in money, but in manufactured goods. Thi
Every president of a cheese factory knows that t
er never yet said :—" I will not buy your chee
take dress goods in pay." No, he gave him a
Bank.

But to resume ; Canada derives her money 1
sells ; in other words, from the amount of cash sh
the sale of her experts to Britain and America.
increase of our trade with Britain depends upon ad
that will cause us to obtain an increased amount (
the total of our European and American export
will also increase the number of our population,
customers. Continental Union will leave Car
same footing as before, as regards the amount
will receive for her trans-Atlantic exports ; and
her to obtain a far larger amount of money fro
her exports for which this continent is the best
sequently, British patriot, if you really desire to ti
fit Britain, advocate the political union of C1
United States, for this policy will, more than any
our population and Britain's customers, and furn
with more money with which to purchase British

MILITARY ADVANTAGES TO BRITAIN

Canada, by uniting her destiny with the
will abolish the many small, but none-the-less in
of friction and war between Britain and Americ
disputable fact that these have in the past often
alarm, and that in the event of war, Canada w
the battle ground.

In the event of Continental Union, Britain,
affairs and powerful on the sea, will retain an
Atlantic and Pacific coasts for naval stations. T

will not object, for Britain is our parent. Who is afraid of un-provoked injury from his mother? Then, by allowing Bri-tain the privilege of sending across our continent, men and freight, other than arms and munition, she will retain all her present military advantages.

The investigation of the causes of modern warfare is un-speakably sad, yet intensely interesting. Fear has been the principal cause of the recent wars on the Continent of Europe. Tyranny, afraid of the brave and the thinkers, has incited and compelled them to slaughter. Britain, reclining securely be-hind her ramparts of freemen, who beheaded and out-lawed her despots, need not aid the projects of foreign tyrants. The de-sire for the absorption of blacks and their landed property has been the direct or indirect cause of the modern wars of Bri-tain.

Canada, a civilized agricultural country, existing in a thoughtful age, and far removed from the arenas of strife, must have an adequate and worthy motive, before she will arm her citizen soldiers to face death on foreign battle fields. Our Can-ada neither needs nor desires more blacks or their territory; therefore whether we be a colony, an independent nation, or affiliated with the Anglo-Saxons on this Continent, we will not as a nation, aid Britain in her foreign wars for territory. But Continental Union being consummated, if ever Britain, driven from her outposts, was receding with her troops across our Continent to defend her heart, we, the hardy sons of the North, would, to a man, spring to arms, and carrying the great Anglo-Saxon Confederacy with us, together pour out our b ood and treasure like water, to defend our common mother,—dear old England. The Anglo-Saxons united are unconquerable and irresistible. Only internecine war can ever break their power.

The United States is now, and will be for centuries, the most powerful military nation on land in the world. Because, in addition to the splendid fighting material to be drawn from her immense population, she is also virtually in command of half of the warriors of Europe. Time, the wonder worker, will cause the pension list to fade away, but the centuries, as they roll by, will still proclaim the unparalled generosity of our Re-publican relatives to the armed citizens, who freed their fellow-men and saved their country. Europe is an armed camp filled with men whose trade is war, and whose highest ambition is military glory. The first tap of the war-drum on American soil will be answered by a million warriors in Europe. The reverberations of the first cannon will not have passed away be-, fore these men will be hastening to the States. They know, that upon entering the army they will be presented with an overflow- ing purse, which a lifetime of labor in Europe would not refill. While in the army, they will be sure of liberal treatment and deserved promotion. When disbanded, they will live a life of ease amid a grateful people. If they meet a soldier's fate, and fall with their faces to the foe, they will be wrapped in a man- tle of glory, by an admiring nation ; and their loved ones will treasured in homes, to them, of luxury. This generosity of the United States, unparalleled in the history of the world, has also been an act of the deepest policy and most profound statesman- ship, for it has made the warriors of the world their own, and the world knows it.

Fellow-citizens will you compare population statistics, and then you will realize that the Greater Britain is, even to-day, not in Europe, but in America. It is your duty as well as in- terest to promote the unity of feeling of the two great divisions of the Anglo-Saxon family,—Great Britain in Europe and the Greater Britain in America.

Continental Union is the first great and only practicable advance, towards forming an offensive and defensive alliance of this dominant race of the globe, whose moral and military pow- er will guarantee perpetual peace to the world-wide, free na- tions of Britons. Therefore, British patriots, from a financial and military standpoint, advocate Continental Union ; for, with- out lessening Britain's advantages, it will diminish the causes and probability of fratricidal war, guarantee the perpetuity of Britain's power, and by Canada's increased prosperity redound to her glory, as the mother, not of palid dwarfs, but of great, prosperous and filial nations.

II—HATER OF AMERICANS.

Perhaps you are more in favor of Continental Union than either the British or Canadian patriot. For, tell it not loudly, this is a policy of Spoilation. How else than by wresting from America men and money, and diverting them to Canada do we propose to benefit our Canadian homes ?

Come, be practical in your hatred. If you have a neigh- bor you hate, and who entices away your sons, and you mutter vapid curses against him, you merely irritate yourself, without injuring your enemy. But, if by forming a partnership with

sell him stones, valuless to you, for good money;
s boats and fish ; get him to pay your crushing
'our sons; sell him corner lots at big prices; and
ee not to intermeddle with your old homestead,—
l farm; you would welcome the partnership, be-
ild benefit yourself at his expense.

III.—CANADIAN PATRIOTISM.

patriot, with relief we turn to you. True
ove for the land in which we earn our bread :
nd of which our bodies form a part; love for our
se therein sheltered ; and actions that will ensure
of the present, and the future, happiness, peace
Canadians, actuated solely by these motives, let
with no half measures, only with the full, im-
ermanent advantages offered by Continental
g the courage of our convictions, let us speak out
nfully.
patriots, you are the decendants, mentally and
the old Gallic heroes, invincible Celts, indomitable
and fearless Norse Vikings, who in the olden
he attribute of courage. You are the off-spring
10 in later times, defending the right, faced heavy
hard fought battle-fields. Knowing that you
ots of heroes, you will not permit yourselves to
ag slaves of cowardice, but will intrepidly utter
nvictions in favor of the policy that will be the
ur Canada. Reason sanctions, and the love of your
es urges you to speak out the truth boldly. Like
orefathers you will hew to the line of rectitude
hips fall where they may. The off-shoots of
not be slaves to cowardice.
lly, to succeed in your private business, you ex-
governed by hard practical common sense, and
spade. Only the same course of action will en-
' to a nation. If you desire your country to take
sition among the free nations of this Continent,
uct the business of your nation on a thoroughly
not striving against the inevitable, but seizing
g advantages.
ieve that if our " Chieftain " were with us, he
y scan the political horizon, seize the right mo-

ment, and, bowing gracefully to the inevita
with flying colors into the harbor of safety
Continental union being acomplished,
towards. Britain will be increased, for Can.
ful to the mother who, to benefit her daug
her union with her big and prosperous rela
ing of amity, which will always exist in Cr
existed in the Southern States, will permea
Great Confederacy. Then America, the Gr
ing out the right hand of friendship to t
Europe, and stretching out the left hand to
will march forward in the van of peace and

IMPERIAL FEDE

IMPERIAL PARLIAMENT AND ITS F

Imperial Federation is the military co
Britain and her Colonies into one empire.
Canada now possesses every right and
separate nation, except the untrammeled po
treaties. Therefore, she could gain no ne
through federation. The people of Canac
being too expensively governed. Federatic
the rulers and the expenses. The tendency
the power and money in the higher gove
allowing each province to exercise full Leg
tive powers over its internal affairs, and to
the bulk of the funds contributed by it
tendency of Federation would be to increas
In proportion to the variation from the
presentation. according to population in t

— 35 —

nent would be more or less an oligarchy. All
their very construction unjust,— conse-
•ry and transient. The majority in the
blacks, the ratio being about six blacks to
ı, both black and white, have equal political
. true has been demonstrated beyond all
; United States it cost, however, one million
and millions of money to prove it. Canada
:st in this problem. Consequently, either
nciple of Imperial federation is unjust, or
t numbered six to one, will be the political

Free Canada does not wish to be affiliated
great majority of which are blacks, and
ide in the history of this continent, either
ving blacks, or being enslaved by them.
any interest in Britain's foreign policy.
ory than we can utilize and have no need or
re, consequently in no event will we aid
ıd money in her wars, for the purpose of
ks and their territory, into the Empire.
ıed no glory upon Canada, and be of no
benefit to her. One citizen of the neigh-
; more than a dozen Asiatics and Africans.
whom we wish to deal, there are more in
ıan in all the British Empire. Considering
ons of blacks and whites in the British Em-
States, the ratio is 40 blacks in the Empire
States.
der, the child of a white mother, prefer be-
›ire, essentially black ? If you do, then by
Imperial Federation.
ederalists propose that the expenses of the
the support, in men and money, of the
.vy be borne *pro rata* by all the nations of
They propose to minimize the representa-
the imperial Parliament. Consequently; the
ıe British Isles, being the majority, would
ar whenever it suited the sole interests of
vould have the silent privilege of paying
s foreign war expenses.
ld demur against this the Canadian Feder-
›ensation to her the commercial advantages
h however, are, in reality, only a great in-

jury to both Britain and Canada.

The commercial policy of the Canadi
been declared to be impracticable by the Fe
and Australia, and is not sanctioned by tl
will investigate it.

RESULTS TO BRITAIN

The Imperial Federalists of Canada pro
no duty on goods going from one componer
pire to another, but duties against all outsid

Britain could not agree to this. This p
at the root of her greatness, which consists i
the sea—the carrier and trader of the comm
The world's goods enter England free of dut
is the world's store house, and the universal
bying and selling, and her ships have the ca
of the globe. Circumscribe her free trade,
vanishes.

The people of Britain know this policy
price of their food and cause great suffering
of her poor, who are now only a few mea
Bread ! Bread ! has been the constant dema
the time of the Roman *panes*, and the Frei
the present day. Britain, powerful and wo
be, knows full well she dare not arouse this

The factories of England, employing 23
population, hold the balance of power in their
their Unions, virtually govern Britain. Brea
the cost of manufacturing. Therefore incre
food would cause an increase in the cost
This would injure Britain in the keen comp
meet in the markets of the world. This wo
more than her colonies benefit her. The p
rather than agree to pay more for their food
charge more for their goods, would let the
now state they will not pamper the colonies
their allegiance.

Judging the future from the past, this
will never be adopted. The CORN-LAWS
and for all time in the history of Britain. Sh
England has not since, and dare not now
tariffs in favor of even her own food produ

favor of ours.

RESULTS TO CANADA.

Even if the proposed policy of the Canadian Imperial Federalists were carried into effect, it would not result in any appreciable advantage to Canadians on the exports to Britain If the duties were so arranged in favor of Canadian food exports that we realized an advance of 10 per cent on the $20,000,-000 worth of food we send to Britain, it would amount to $2,-000,000. Just an increased profit of fifty cents a piece to Canadians. This famine tainted half-dollar would be blood money, carrying a curse with it. What Canadian would desire to obtain his solitary half-dollar, wrung from the hunger of the children of the poor in Britain?

The policy of the Canadian Imperial Federalist, instead of being a financial benefit to Canada, would be a serious injury. Granted that we obtain 10 p. c. advance on our exports to Britain, we would have to pay 10 per cent. advance on the price of our English imports. On account of the extra price of food it would be necessary for the English manufacturers, in order to recoup themselves, to charge 10 per cent. advance on former prices. As British goods would pay no duties on entering Canada, English manufacturers could and would charge us within a trifle of the price that other foreign goods, which paid duty, cost laid down in Canada, and yet be able to retain our custom. Therefore, British goods would cost us in our stores nearly the same prices as before Federation.

The loss will now appear. The money obtained from the present duties furnishes a large part of our revenue. Under Federation the duties on British imports would be cut off. An increased revenue, in the event of Federation, would require to be raised, for in addition to our present expenditure, there would be our proportion of the expenditure of the Empire. Hence, we would be compelled to raise by direct taxation or other means, a larger amount than our present duty on imports from Great Britain, in order to make good this deficiency in the revenue. So our loss by this policy would be an amount equal to the present duty on British imports, plus our proportion of the Imperial expenditure. All the present numerous custom houses would be retained, and the expenses of many would exceed the duties collected.

The consequences to Canada of this policy would be as disastrous as to Great Britain. Allowing British goods to enter Canada free of duty would increase smuggling all along the 4,-00 miles of the American border line. The bitterest of feelings would ensue between the Canadian and American Governments. The United States, possessing the products of every clime, does not require any Canadian products. The American Government would enforce a double prohibitory tariff—both import and ex-

port. Canada along 4,000 miles would be boycotted. Our tv
great R. R's. have both their head and feet on American so
These would be amputated. Our population now deserts us
the rate of 300 daily. Food would be dearer in Canada than
the United States. The exodus would increase to a 1000 dail
The few who remained would supplicate for Annexation upo
any terms. Rancor would exact an unconditional surrender..

Away with such a policy as Imperial Federation. Cana
wants none of it. We desire no policy that will injure eith
ourselves or Great Britain. Cinadians can make money witl
out being under compliments to any nation. We wi
not make it, by extracting it from the hungry of our kin i
Europe.

All we ask is a fair field and no favors. A fair field we nev
have had. Our hands have been tied to Europe and by Eu
ope, so that we have not had free interchange with the gre
nations, our relatives in North America. Let us once be fre
handed and inside the ring of free nations on our continent an
they will have to look to their laurels. We will equal if n
surpass the best of them. Physically we are their superior
Mentally, more enduring. Ask the employers of brain an
muscle in the Western states if they do not select their en
ployees in accordance with this proven fact?

Let Canadians, while their country is yet solvent, propo
union upon equal terms with the other free nations of the gre
American Confederacy. Their commerce stands now upon th
same footing in Europe as ours. Therefore, by Continent
Union, Canada will not lose any advantage in the Europea
markets, but gain those of America, which are of more impor
ance to her. America is the only market for many of our pr
ducts.

If it were necessary for Canada to choose between bein
totally bebarred from Europe or America, and it were left sol
ly to her monetary interests to decide, the verdict would be i
favor of having America as a free market, because the additio
al population that free trade with the United States would em
ploy in our mines, forests and lakes, would consume more tha
our present exports to Britain. But the time for this decisio
will never come. Canada does not intend to enter into politic
union with the United States without the consent of Britain.

Under Continental Union, Canada will still be as loyal t
Britain as ever. If remaining at home, where he was no assist
ance, caused a son to be poor in blood and pocket,would the so
love the father less, because he allowed him to accept a remun
erative, healthful and honorable position with his relatives
Canadians, in the interests of Britain, of Canada, and of ou
race, advocate the policy that injures none and benefits all
Continental Union.

CANADIAN FARMERS

————o————

;URES CONCERNING AGRICULTURE THAT ARE
WORTHY OF CONSIDERATION.

s of Canada deserve equal chances for properity
e States. *These they have never had.*
illustrate this, permit it to be supposed, kind
writer and yourself are two farmers who live
s of the same town line. You are the Canadian
on the north side of the town line, in a town-
ida. I am the American farmer and live on
other township called the States. Personally,
ood friends, but the two township councils, for
i private interests, are often unfriendly. You
wheat and cattle to a distant market called
here is great competition. There we both get
neither of us having to pay any market dues.
oose, that the best place at which to sell our
bs is at a market in my township called the
et. I can sell there at full price without paying
s. But, when you drive on the American mar-
and lambs, are charged market dues that come
ir value. Your produce is charged these dues
: on the north side of the town line. The buyers
market dues,and give you two-thirds of the price

g the circumstances, would you consider, Can-
iat you realize as much for your labor as I, the
er, do for mine ? Could you make as much
ur farm as I ? Do not these market dues benefit
ownship at your expense ? Would a reduction
lues satisfy you ? Would you not be afraid that
l between the two township councils would re-
ket dues being raised higher than ever ? The
wnships would cause you and I to stand on the
the markets of both Britain and America,
is paying market dues in either place. Would
han this union satisify you ? Would not the

ratepayers in your township elect councillors who would favd this union of the townships? If this is the wisest course adopt in township affairs, it is also in national affairs. Conti ental Union will give the Canadian farmer equal advantag with the American. It would be the duty of the ratepayers a township to advocate a political policy which would benefit their township alone. If the same policy would benefit all t thousand townships of a country, its benefits are a thousan fold. Therefore, the duty of the patriots of that country, advocate this policy,is a thousand times greater than the simil obligation resting upon the ratepayers, of a single townshi which would be benefited by a local policy.

The Canadian farmer may prove to his satisfaction that l is the loser on account of, and to just the amount of the Amei can duty on his produce that goes to the States. The meth to pursue would be as follows:—Let him find out the pla at which his produce enters the States, or the name of the pla in the States the nearest to his residence where the same cla of produce is raised. Then, get a newspaper from there, th contains the prices that are obtained by the American farm in that locality. Let the Canadian farmer then compare pric and he will know that he has paid the freight and duty. Tl freight he ought to pay, but he has been defrauded out of tl duty by continental isolation, perpetuated by selfish politician Continental Union is the only logical and permanent remed for continental isolation.

Now, for some hard reliable facts, regarding the pro lu of our farms. The following statistics are taken from the Sta tistical year books of Canada for 1889, 1890 and 1891, publis ed by the Department of Agriculture, and printed by the Gov ernment Printing Bureau at Ottawa. These books are tl highest official documents of statistics that are published by ou Dominion, and they are especially intended for the guidance our Parliaments:

BARLEY.
Exported from Canada to

United States		Britai
1889	$ 6,454,603	$ 3,83
1890	4,582,563	12,01
1891	2,849,269	75,22

Statistics prove that the greater part of this barley was th product of Ontario. The farmers of this province will observ with sorrow, that the difference, between the total amounts fo

:y in 1891 and 1889, was $3,500,000. This
:o the McKinley Bill, which caused less bar-
.a far lower price to be obtained for it.
ff the duty entirely, would cause more bar-
d the price to be far higher.
e principal market for barley, in the Bay of
ie average price there, was in 1889, 75 cents
. But a sailing vessel would in a few hours
)swego, where the price was in 1892, 75
:ontinental isolation prevents the Canadian
ing the same price for his barley, that is re-
er in N. Y. State for barley, which is on the
Is it not strange that this is true at the close
entury, when all men consider they are free
entitled to equal remuneration for similar

ithstanding the American duty of 30 cents
greater portion of our barley was bought by
This proves that the unspeakably detestable
illing to pay us 30 cents more a bushel for
han the malster or stockman of "Dear old
is that business is devoid of sentiment, and
ips.
in farmers could get 30 cents a bushel more
id do not use the means to obtain it, does it
y are more loyal to strangers in Britain,
he loved ones sheltered within their own

h nor American farmers would thus al-
be enslaved by prejudice and robbed by poli-

WHEAT.

Exported by Canada to
	Britain
....................................$	439,863
....	379,893
....	969,134

the yield of wheat for 1891, with that of any
must recollect that in this year, many thous-
i prairie in Manitoba and the North-west
or the first time sown with wheat. Almost
xported in 1891 from Canada to Britain was
h West. This remark also applies to the
's that succeed 1891.

The farmers of Manitoba desire to obta
tion immediataly, and not after all the p:
dead. An increased population means to th(
bridges; larger home markets; more schools,
and all this with a reduced taxation. They
chase their machinery and other manufac
prices paid in the States which are fro
cheaper. They especially wish a reduction
freight on wheat. The map of North A1
solution of the question : " How to send the
Europe at the lowest possible freight rates.'
be sent by rail only as far as the head of nava;
highways should be opened up, so that the o
load at Port Arthur,and sail without breaking
ain. Continental Union will furnish Manitob
tion and lower the prices of freight and mac
policy will do this. Canada cannot afford t
highway and the Republic wil not do it, w
the St. Lawrence. But union will cause th
confederacy for the sake of all the north h1
to develop to the fullest extent, the water hi;
lakes and the St. Lawrence river and thu
ports of the great lakes into ocean ports.
be derived from this are incalculable.

When the Ontario farmer heard that
would lower the price of his barley, he so
more wheat, believing that Britain would 1
and so enable him to realize as much as
But in this he was woefully mistaken. Fo
with surprise, that while the exports of
States were in 1890 only $6,000, they were
of a million dollars, which means about on
wheat. This was principally the wheat 1
tunate Ontario farmer, which Britain had ε
·buy, unless she could purchase it for cattle
same price she had payed for his barley. '
that the Ontario farmer was obliged to sell
at runinously low prices. This was becaus
tion imposed a duty of 25 cents a bushel o
it could have access to the markets of its o·
greater part of this Ontario wheat was gr(
Western wheat in the Eastern States, and c(
ly by exiles from the Province of Quebec, ·

s in the factories of the New England States. This shows how inseparable are our business connections with the Unit-ed States, and how our American cousins extricate us out of a difficulty, when our unfounded faith in the markets of Britain has misled us.

Let us now ascertain the total loss on barley and wheat to-gether, that the McKinley Bill caused to the Ontario farmers in 1891 compared with 1889. You recollect they expected the in-creased amount of money they would receive from their wheat would compensate them for the loss on the barley. Take your pencil and add together all the barley money of 1889, and that portion of the wheat money which was exported in 1889 to the United States. Then seperately add together all the barley money of 1891, and that portion of the wheat money which was export-ed in 1891 to the United States, which was the soft wheat of On-tario. Subtract the total of 1891 from that of 1889 and over $3,000,000 is before you. This loss to the Ontario farmers on a total of their barley and wheat of $3,000,000 was caused by this bill closing the door through which trade passes between Canada and the States, a little tighter. Will you then estimate how much they would gain on the total receipts from the ex-ports of their barley and wheat, if Continental Union took commerce excluding door off its hinges, and broke it up, so that it could never be rehung. Would it not be at least $5,000,-000 annually?

Get a Canadian year-book from your Dominion member of parliament, and see for yourself that these startling figures are correct.

WHEAT CROP OF THE WORLD, 1891.

United States	.612 million bushels	
British India	255 "	"
Russia	169 "	"
Austria	167 "	"
Canada	61 "	"
Argentine Republic	33 "	"
Australia	33 "	"

But, compare, with surprise :—

Great Britain bought in 1891 from

United States	62½ million bushels	
Russia	36½ "	"
British India	17 "	"
Roumania	9 "	"

Did you think Romania sold Britain twio
as Canada ?

CHEESE.

But some say, if the Americans sell Brit
wheat for Canada's one, Canada sells Britain 1
cheese, while the States only sell her 87 mi
average Canadian cheese is superior to the ᴜ
Here is the reason : No cheese made after Se]
is sent out of the United States. The fall chee
best, are eaten in the Republic, and only the s]
cheese are sent to England. Besides, the maj
tories in some of the Western States never
cheese to Britain ; their cheese is sent to tl
South Eastern States. Canada, as a nation, se
it because her children can not afford to eat it
the United States are numerous and wealthy ε
bulk of their cheese. Only a small proportioɪ
cheese is sent across the ocean ; the best rema
because the Americans pay far better prices foɪ
than the British. Thus, Canada looses heav
through being deprived of her share of the ma
tinent. The loss to the Canadian farmers on
account of not being able to sell them in the
over a million dollars annually.

In fact, continuing to imagine that Cε
Europe, and not of America, costs each Canadi
on an average $300,00. He gains nothing, ab
in recompense. His allegiance to Britain does
even favorable consideration. When he visiɪ
astonishment, he realizes that an Americaɪ
highly esteemed there than a Canadian. A Cε
sider is only a colonist, living in a dependent
onto England's apron. Whereas an Americaɪ
of one of the greatest nations of the world, an
he may some day be the President of the ᴘ
thus the equal of the Queen of England her
tinent of Europe the respect for an American
yet. A wealthy American, on registering

y as "John I. King, of Chicago, U. S. A.," was addressed by
obsequious landlord as " Your Majesty, John the First, King
hicago."

CATTLE

The farmers in Canada, east of Toronto, lose on both their
k and fat cattle, on account of not having free access to the
kets of the neighboring States. Beef and stock cattle are
iys higher in the eastern part of New York State than in
adjacent parts of Ontario. Quebec and the Eastern Pro-
es lose largely on their cattle by being excluded from the
se manufacturing districts of the adjacent New England
es. Therefore, the eastern part of Canada suffers serious
icial injury in the cattle trade by continental isolation. This
usion from the markets of our continent, results from our
:ical connection with Britain.

Cattle, sheep and horse dealers try to ship when the mar-
is on the rise, Britain being distant, the price there has
: in which to fall before the stock arrives. Consequently,
· few Canadian dealers,who continuously shipped to England,
ɔ eventually realized much, if anything, from their business.
:reas the dealers can place their stock upon the American
kets,in nearly as many hours as it takes days to go to Eng-
l ; consequently, the markets there are surer, and more of
shippers to the States have accumulated wealth.

An American farmer has the choice of markets. He can
without paying duty, either to the 65 millions at home or
he 40 millions in Britain—a total of about 105 millions. The
adian farmer has his 5 millions in Canada and the 40 mil-
s in Britain—a total of about 45 millions. Therefore, the
ket of the Canadian farmer is not half as large, as that of
farmer in the States.

The Canadian lives in hopes of having a larger population
)anada to supply. This generation will never see 65 millions
ig in Canada. Why not accept the immediate opportunity,
applying the 65 millions at home next door, on our contin-
? For many products the American market is better than
British, because an American, when he is thoroughly satisfi-
vith an article, will pay a higher price than a man of any
ɔr nationality.

To come to facts, a sensible farmer likes to sell where he
sell the best. His own prosperity is of more importance
iim, than either or both of the political parties of the day ;
it does not put any money in or out of his pocket, whether
head man in the country, is called the president, or the

Governor-General, and that is about all the rea
is between the Canadian and American Govern

SHEEP.

In 1892, the United States bought from
sheep and lambs, whereas Britain purchased
us. The American duty on sheep is $1.50,
cents each. Figure for yourself, how many
lambs Canada would raise, and how much
would receive for them, if political union took
American tariff sheep barriers.

· Canada has immense areas of unoccupie
adapted for sheep culture. Near and profitabl
cause these hills to be covered with flocks, ten
ed shepherds. Sheep raising would develop
great and most profitable industries, and we
annual export of sheep and lambs, not by
millions.

The mutton of the Scottish sheep is m
than the English. The same is true as regard
ton, when compared with the American. Our
bors earn and spend more money than any
and willingly pay a good price for a savory di
epicurean tastes. Therefore, the Canadian m
command ready sales at highly remunerativ
United States. Canadians, it will pay you
and grind to powder, the American tariff wa
riers.

HORSES.

Since Confederation, Canada has exporte
of that number the United States bought 32
adian farmers made the wealthy Republic a
000 in duties, for the privilege of selling these
the above figures conclusively prove to be
natural horse market. No matter what the p
the farmer does not relish the duty of $30 or
that is imposed by the McKinley Bill. For
does not relish any duty on any product of hi
observing his own common-sense actions in h
telligent farmer can learn how to avoid havin
farm produce reduced, by an American tari
ceives one of his horses is about to kick, if he
the reach of injury altogether, he simply spri
horse that no ill effects can result. Contin
bring the Canadian farmer so close to the Uni

1 be impossible for any American tariff to hurt him. Horse
se is in favor of Continental Union. It is to your interest
ote for the union of Canada and the States.

Many farmers have wondered, why the British Govern-
nt did not purchase Canadian horses for the army, when
ey are suitable for many army purposes, and we are willing
sell them so cheap, Here is the real reason :—The English
orse breeders objected so vehemently, that the British Govern-
nt dared not buy them. You can ascertain this to be an in-
sputable fact, by reading page 297 of the Canadian year-
ok for 1891. In the item of horses alone, so called loyalty to
European power has cost the farmers of Canada $7,000,000,
d this large sum did not come out of the official class, who
e loyal to their fat salaries, but it was wrung from the toil of
e hard working farmers—the tax payers of this country, not
e tax eaters. And yet, when the opportunity offered, they
re debarred from selling their horses to the Government for
ich they had sacrificed $7,000,000 on this very product of
ir farms. This proves that when the interests of the British
mer, clash with those of the Canadian farmer, the colonist
s to go to the wall every time. This also shows that the far-
rs of Canada are less loyal to themselves, than the farmers of
tain, who practise one of the first principles of business,
ich is to specially regard their own interests. The British
mers tell the Canadian farmers, by acst which speak far
der than words, to look out for their own interests, for they
determined to look out for theirs.

It is high time for the farmers of Canada to enquire and
re for themselves, which policy will best serve their own in-
sts, and the interests of those dependent upon them. The
ority of the voters in Canada are farmers, therefore, when
farmer advocates the policy that he knows will enrich
self personally, he is also promoting the prosperity of his
try.

EGGS.

Exported by Canada to

ted States.	Britain.
$2,156,725	$ 18
1,793,104	820
1,074,247	83,589
494,409	592,218

You will observe that Canada received twice as much
ey for her export of eggs in 1889 as she did in either 1891 or
. This loss was caused by the Americans refusing to al-

low the Canadian eggs to come into the United States fr
duty. How dependent Canada is upon the good will of
United States for a market for half of her farm prod
British allegiance does not bestow upon us a single favor in
British markets; her markets are as open and as favorabl
Japan as to Canada.

The egg statistics show that Britain stopped short
way, and did not come fully to the rescue of even our hens,w
the McKinley hawk frightened them. British allegiance
the women of Canada in both 1891 and 1892 one million
lars each year on their egg money, for the McKinley Bill
not charge a duty of 5 cents a dozen on the price of eggs la
by American hens in the United States. The American I
pay best. Ladies,you had better change the breed of your h
and then you will get twice as much money for your eggs.
only way to get this extra pocket money, is by advising yu
husbands to vote for the union of Canada and the States.

HAY.
Exported by Canada to

United States.		Brit
1889	$822,381	$ 84.
1890	922,797	109,
1891	375,813	150,
1892	598,567	167,

When the McKinley Bill was passed the politicians fa
fully promised that Britain would come to the aid of Cana
and buy all our hay. " Never mind the Americans," they s
" Britain will take all our hay and pay us good prices." T
was impossible—any school boy could give the reason. Al
one half of our boundary line, he could *throw* a stone fr
Canada into the States. Whereas 3,000 miles of the expanse
the Atlantic intervene between Canada and Britain.

It is impossible to ship our cheap and bulky farm p
ducts to the British markets, and be able to realize a remun
ative price. because the heavy ocean freights cut the Canad
price down to almost nothing. Therefore, Canadians prefered
pay the excessive American duty, and ship the bulk of th
hay to the adjacent markets of our continent, as is proven
the above statistics. The freight across our great lakes av
ages one dollar a ton for pressed hay, and the price of hay l
often been $5.00 higher on the American side of the lakes, a
rarely ever less than $3.00 higher. The prices for Canadi
hay at New York and Liverpool do not generally differ ve
much. The freight from Canada to Liverpool is stated; by t

'eb. 2nd, 1893, to be $13.50 per ton for pressed
Ontario and Quebec to New York it is from
Our Quebec farmers receive about $4.00 a ton
s sent to England. This pays them low wages
id nothing for their hay.
may sound to Canadians, even our best
t a favorite in England. Their climate,
tion and variety of seed are all different, con-
is different, they appreciate their own article
not pay full prices for our hay. Whereas,
preciable difference between the hay grown in
Northern States, our hay, when of good quality,
rices in New York City.
ds of pressed hay, bought at $6.00 a ton, were
ov. and Dec., 1892, from Napanee station to
where the price was then from $17.00 to $20.00,
ty. The duty was $4.00, the freight was $3.50
profit to the dealer of from $4.50 to $6.50 a
iinental Union the farmers would have re-
price $6.00 plus the duty $4.00, which equals
s no farmer to sell a ton of hay for less. Only
ipelled the industrious Napanee farmers to
ay that was worth at least $10.00 to them to
arms. Agriculturists, advocate the policy that
id of $6.00 for farm produce.

1MON-SENSE ARGUMENTS.

pon the American market for the sale of those
iat Britain does not need, or can buy more
. Canada has never been under any com-
n. Seeming compliments invariably coincided
iterests, and if her interests had so dictated,
granted as readily to Madagascar as to Can-
ind everything of equal value sent from Russia,
iited States, command exactly the same prices
rkets. Continental Union would leave our
upon exactly the same footing as before, and
eely, fully and permanently the American
re by far the best for some of our agricultural

ns tell the Canadians that the farmers in the
well off as those in Canada; therefore, they
union will not benefit Canadians. We need to
order to make fair comparisons it is necessary
of each country, that are equal in date of

settlement, character of settlers, and quality of
ticians do not do this,.but compare some ne
peopled with raw foreign settlers, with an old
purposely forgetting that our pioneers also ha
from the bottom of the ladder. Canadians are
workers than Yankees, and the soil in the ir
Canada is 20 per cent more productive than tl
so we ought to be far richer than any State in
are not. The States have nearly paid off their
age ; ours is growing yearly. Consequently w
than we really are ; they poorer. When our n
to be paid, and that time will soon come, the
the burden will,as usual, fall upon the farmers.
al Union will enable them to evade this
union would cause our heavy Dominion and Pi
be assumed by the whole of the new confede
would only have to pay one fourteenth of it,ins
000,000 we are now in debt.

The wealth of the United States has in
since 1860. Has the community in the pa
which you reside increased in wealth four-fold i
The average price of the ordinary necessities
cent cheaper in the United States than in Cana
tion of the United States debt since March 1
lions, which is just the amount of the Car
debt.

Now for some Government statistics, wl
prosperity of the States with that of Britain,
ada :—
Total wealth of the United States...........
        "   "   " Britain....................
Yearly output of all the factories of United State
        "   "   "   "   "   Britain......
American production of the world's iron, 1892
British   "   "   "   "   "   " .
Earnings of the American people, 1887.......
        "   "   "   British   "   "   ....
        "   "   "   French   "   "   ....
Bank circulation per family in Canada 1891...
        "   "   "   "   " United States...
U. S. all agricultural exports 1892...........
Canada all   "   "   1892...........
Total rail-road mileage of all Canada.........
        "   "   "   " just one State (Illin

Canadian farmers, the remedy for the disadvantages under
ich you labor is in your hands to apply or not as you see fit.
No man can be more diligent or exercise more shrewdness
comm on sense in his private and local affairs than the Can-
in agriculturist. This is shown by his comparative pros-
ity, even when deprived of a free market for the American
f of his farm produce, and by the decided ability displayed
farmers in the management of the business of our county
ncils. The great majority of the noted men of our contin-
including all the ablest presidents of colleges, railroads, and
he great Republic, have been the sons of farmers.
The majority of the voters of Canada are engaged in agri-
ural pursuits. This being the case, the majority of the mem-
s of our parliaments ought to be farmers—men who would
rcise the same diligence and common-sense in the interests
griculture in the Provincial and Dominion Halls that they
n private and local affairs. Canada has to-day among her
ners, patriotic men who are intelligent, well informed, and
essed of great practicable ability. Farmers possessing these
lities have, in all ages of the world, been the men who con-
ed the greatest benefits upon their countries. Who was
1 Hampden, the great champion of English liberty, the
st man of his age? He was an intelligent farmer. Hear
words of another farmer, also of English extraction, who,
n resigning the position of Commander-in-chief of his nation,
:—" I commend the interests of our dearest country to the
ction of Almighty God,and those who have the superinten-
e of them, to His holy keeping." These were the words of
hington, who was first a farmer, then a great general, then
reatest statesman the British nation has produced,and then
1 a farmer. Would not farmers like these manage the
ness of our nation as well as those glib speakers we send
e legislative halls?
The farmers of Canada have sent men to Parliament who
their callings in life were not in sympathy with the great
stry of Canada—agriculture. These men have usurped
brity, and have become the rulers,instead of the servants of
ountry, and forced policies upon us that have assisted in
ucing the present financial depression. Has the time not
when the farmers—the back-bone of Canada--will send
to Parliament who will not attempt to rule their fellow
ns, but to faithfully represent them and their interests?
ers, the destiny of Canada, for weal or woe, is in your
s!

Some object to a union with the States
morality. Many of these objectors have valic
if they had lived in the States instead of in C
have been, before now, imprisoned on accoul
general rascality. Others, who are really goc
their eyes to the crimes committed in Canad:
to those committed in the States, and object t
class have never made a study of States rig
had, they would know that each State legisla
al and marriage laws, commands the executiv
obedience to them and to punish the crimi:
them. This would place greater power than
of each province to further the interests of :
would cease to be a dumping ground for the
Britain, and would naturally attract the thr
migrants of Britain and Northern Europe.
a question of climate, therefore Canada will
gards morality, the Britain and Scandinavia

The respected clergy of Canada must adi
al Union would give an immense *impetus* t
ligion. The wealthier portion of every oi
denominations is in the Republic. This polic
the Canadian churches. Christianity in C
wealth, because, it is the comparatively hea
direct taxation of our churches, that is chiefl
rapidly lose their grasp upon the masses. T
colleges, the ablest-teachers, and the most bri
thinkers, of all these denominations, are in t
fore, the complete union, which would be
union, of the weaker portions of these denom:
with the abler and stronger in the United St
ed strength to the cause of religion in Canac
wealth, this infusion of new blood, and this
tians of this continent, in order to oppose th
infidelity, who now preaches to the half &
who are at the present time practically outsi

No well grounded arguments can be adv
tinental Union. It is not disloyal; because t
ain will first be obtained before it will be :
Only lawful, constitutional and peaceful i
use of by its advocates to influence the Can
voters of Canada when convinced of its bene
bers of Parliament who favor it. When its i
majority in our Parliaments, Canada will req

sanction the reunion of the Anglo-Saxons of
Vhen it receives their consent, the man will
poses Continental Union by any unconstitu-
the advocates of this policy will from first to
mally, they can never be disloyal.
s adoption cause Canada to receive one dollar
tlantic exports. The products of all the
id the same prices in the British markets.
ives the consent of Britain to her alliance
tons of this continent, our products will still
prices in the British markets as those of the
As regards the advantages of this policy to
of agriculture, no farmer needs to be inform-
or barley to sell—or cotton,coal oil or machin-
prosperity of Canada depends almost solely
y of the agricultural population. Hence each
by advocating a policy which he knows will
also aiding his country, Every intelligent
free access to all the markets of this con-
him. Continental Union will bestow this
rpetually and no other policy will do this.
ill also effect an immense saving in the ex-
our governments. Over one half of our
ment and custom officials will be dismissed.
expect that some of these parties will be op-
. It is amusing to notice that the violence of
enerally in exact proportion to the fatness of their
ascertaining the amount of the salary or per-
these gentlemen, we can easily estimate the
position to political union,without the trouble
ech.
n politicians, about election time, promise
cted, they will give the farmers free trade
tates. Do not believe them. They cannot
, and they know it. Canadian farmers change
nerican statesman. Imagine yourself an
honestly desiring to benefit the United Stat es
ire to benefit any other country in the world.
as feeling responsible for the prosperity
our fellow citizens with all their eyes upon
ture the Great Republic, containing every
l the product of every clime, thus forming
dependent world—independent alike of Can-
ions on the north, and Mexico with its 10

millions on the south-west. Would you, as an American par
extend to alien Canada, often disagreable Canada, any adv
age at the expense of the United States ? Now hear the tr
The power to grant or refuse reciprocity is vested solely in
statesmen of the great Republic. Their actions in this matter
be entirely governed by the interests of the United States, w
out any reference whatever to those of Canada. This is comr
sense.

Come, let us go to little children and learn the policy o
United States towards Canada. Fourteen little children l
isolated in a new settlement called America. Thirteen little
built a playhouse and merrily gathered their toothsome mo
within it. One peevish child, with covetous eyes, had s
aloof throughout. "Give me," said she, "a share of your t
sures, and I will run away with them and enjoy them al
myself." Those who are inside desire their cousin to join tl
Now, what will they say ? Will it not be in substance thi
"If we did not wish you to come in, we might out of g
nature give you a part. But we know if we share with
while you stand outside, you will have gained all that en
you to enter, so you will not come into our playhouse. Th
fore. you will get no favors from us until you join us, and t
we will generously share equally with you." Credit the Am
cans with knowing as much as a child six years old.

They desire us to come into their union. We desire
financial benefits to be derived from free access to their mark
This is the bait with which to allure Canada to join them
they know it. They also know that if they give us their n
kets, free of duty, we will have acquired from them all we
sire ; consequently we will not join their union. They withl
these benefits from us, retaining them for their own people,
are the only ones just entitled to them. When we join th
they will share with us but not before.

But some, not yet convinced, say :—Canada once had r
procity with the United States, therefore, she will be able to
it again. To this special part of the subject the writer has gi
great attention, and he has good reasons for making the foll
ing statement :—The principal statesmen of the United St
have no sincere intention to hereafter negotiate any reciproc
treaty with Canada that will be appreciably beneficial to
Their chief reason is simply this :—They know from the exp
ence of the past that kindness on the part of the Republic
not induce Canada to join their union.

Once before in the history of Canada, trade was stagn
money was withdrawn from commerce, the best of the pop

were leaving, and real estate sold for little more than one-
its former value. The consequence was, that many Can-
ins desired a political alliance with the United States. The
public granted us reciprocity, foolishly thinking that kind-
would win over the Canadians who yet dissented. What
e the results to Canada? Prosperity immediately ensued
iccount of our trade with the United States increasing from
,000,000 to $80,000,000, and Canada remained loyal not to
own interests but to Europe. The Americans in the mean-
e ascertained that the terms which benefited Canada, did it
heir expense, and that their kindness to Canada had the
.t of causing her to withdraw from political union with them.
the Republic abrogated the treaty and has never renewed it,
ugh often solicited.

The present financial depression is again causing Canadians
nink most seriously, but unfortunately for us the Americans
e learnt their lesson from the experience of the past, and
y never require to be taught the same lesson a second time.
y know that kindness on their part will never cause Canada
oin them, therefore, as long as we remain a part of the British
pire, they will treat us, not unkindly, but merely with utter
fference—just the same as Britain does. They will act to-
ds us the same as they do toward any nation who exports
same products, and give us no advantage whatever on ac-
nt of our relationship—which is again just the same as Brit-
does. This conduct on the part of the United States will
be from any ill-feeling toward us, but from a knowledge
t the pursuance of this course of action will be certain to
mote their interests—both in the present from the duties they
ive from our exports and from the immigration of our
th—and also in the future by making certain our union
h them. They will defer the revelation of their kindly feel-
s for their neighboring northern cousins until we unite with
m. The Americans are well aware of the fact that nothing
the desire to promote our selfish interests will ever cause
ida to agree to political union; consequently they will so
ulate their policy that it will be to our interests to desire
s union.

In order to benefit ourselves, let us join with our American
isins on equal terms, and build up a mighty nation, extending
m the Gulf of Mexico to the Artic circle, and from the shores
the Atlantic to the Pacific Ocean, in which all farmers will
ve the same free markets and enjoy the same privileges.
ur interests are identical with the interests of Canada, so in
vocating political union, you both benefit your homes and act

the part of patriots. Let this policy be ably represented in (
legislative halls. Let the Parliament of Great Britain and
Congress of America sanction it. Then the English speak,
people of America will be one nation, the greatest, richest, a
most intelligent that the world has ever seen; and the two gr
families of Anglo-Saxons will join hands across the Atlantic
a clasp of eternal friendship.

THE PROVINCES AS STATES.

Under Continental Union each Province would retain
name, organize its own internal government, and make an i (
force all its own civil and criminal laws. Our village, tov
city, township and county councils, having been borrowed fr(
the States and not from Britain, would remain as they are
present. It is probable, however, that we would of our o
accord gradually reduce the number of the members of th
councils in accordance with more business-like ideas. The i
jority of the custom houses between Canada and the Uni
States would be abolished. We could, and likely would, ret
our present educational system. Our Provincial parliame
have since Confederation been in all the essentials, Republi(
and not Monarchal, therefore as State parliaments they co
remain unchanged. We are in fact in all our Provincial matt
now Americans and not British, only we do not know it.
would obey the same Provincial laws as we do now. In ad
tion, however, to the present legislative and executive power
our Provincial or State Parliaments,they would have full po\
over the criminal laws and some others. We, and not the F
mier, would probably, though not necessarily, elect the m(
bers of the Provincial or State Cabinet. In the Republi
State Cabinet consists only of a Secretary of State, a St
Treasurer and an Attorney-General, though we could hav
dozen in the cabinet if we wished. Our present Provin
Lieutenant-Governor would be elected by the people; and
called the Governor of Ontario, Quebec, etc. Each province
state could have its own judges, appointed as at present, dec
ing the same cases by the same laws and with the same jur
It is not compulsory upon any state to adopt the elective s
tem of appointing judges. There would be a few Federal jud
in addition,appointed by the House of Representatives,to deci
upon disagreements arising out of foreign treaties, dispu
between states, etc. These we would very rarely come in c(
tact with. In short, each province or state would remain as
is at present, as regards all the essentials of its internal mana\
ment, the only difference would be the increased independer
and legislative and executive powers of our *local provinci*

ch state or province is supposed to look out
itters pertaining to its own business. The United
leracy of numerous, separate and independent
gether for the public good of its citizens.
e provinces would remain undisturbed, the
ra would be startling. The Governor-General
obility, the Commander-in-Chief, the High
London, the Canadian House of Lords alias
'remier and his Cabinet, all the Dominion
ament and all the numerous salaried officials at
e dismissed. These, number over 350; their
ary from $50,000 each, down to the comfort-
$1,000, and mileage, for a few months attend-
ld effect an immense saving to Canada. The
work they now do would be transferred to and
e provincial or state legislatures. The small
ition remaining to be performed would only
sentatives, who would be elected to the House
es of the great Confederacy. This Confeder-
mate to which the parliament of each province
ect two members. By this procedure, we
our characteristics and advantages, and abolish
useless and expensive part of our legislative
· business as a nation would be conducted up-
sis. The electorate would select as our public
st of our citizens. They would be paid only
th the work done, and there would be no fat
ed incapables.

ERRATA.

e 28 treatise instead of treaties.

inexhaustable	" "	unexhaustable.
within sight	" "	inwi thsight.
locate	" "	locat.
duties	" "	doties
United	" "	Uusted.
saw	" "	sawed.
fulfillment	" "	fulfilment.
decide	" "	deside.
exports	" "	experts.
paid	" "	payed.
separately	" "	seperately.
Roumania	" "	Romania.

www.ingramcontent.com/pod-product-compliance
Lightning Source LLC
Chambersburg PA
CBHW021541270326
41930CB00008B/1324